Original title:
Tales of the Great Depths

Copyright © 2025 Creative Arts Management OÜ
All rights reserved.

Author: Simon Fairchild
ISBN HARDBACK: 978-1-80587-442-3
ISBN PAPERBACK: 978-1-80587-912-1

Legends of Lost Horizons

In waters wide where mermaids danced,
A fish wore shoes, and lobsters pranced.
They held a ball, what a sight to see,
With seahorses spinning so merrily!

The octopus played a jazzy beat,
While clams clapped along with their feet.
A whale in a tux, he looked so grand,
But tripped on seaweed, oh wasn't it planned!

The Depths Unveiled

A turtle with glasses read a book,
While eels debated who's the best cook.
The starfish argued, quite loud and bold,
While crabs sold stories of seaweed gold.

A dolphin danced with a parrot's flair,
As bubbles floated through salty air.
Then a shrimp on a surfboard rode by,
Screaming, 'Watch out! I can fly!'

Fables from the Forgotten Sea

A gnome in a shell went fishing for laughs,
With squeeze toy squid and rubbery staffs.
He caught a catfish who sang a tune,
Checkered flounders provided the boom!

The seahorse served popcorn with zest,
While jellyfish played as a light-up guest.
They made a show under moon's soft glow,
And all of the fish gathered to "Whoa!"

Murmurs of the Deep Blue

In dark waters where shadows creep,
A narwhal snored in a cozy heap.
His friends threw fish, oh what a treat,
But he woke up mad and stomped his feet.

A pirate parrot squawked a song,
While sea cucumbers jived along.
They swirled and twirled in silly ways,
As bubbles burst into laughter's plays!

Fables of the Drowned

In waters deep where fish joke and jive,
The mermaids chat while the crabs high five.
With seaweed snacks and bubbles of cheer,
They laugh at the sailors who quiver with fear.

A dolphin's dance turns tides into fun,
As octopuses paint in hues of the sun.
The shark plays cards with a wise old eel,
And everyone knows a squid's great at feel.

Hearts of Lost Mariner

A mariner lost with a map upside down,
Found treasure in starfish, but lost his crown.
He wore a goldfish as a fancy hat,
Exclaiming to crabs, "I'm stylish, look at that!"

He danced with the barnacles under the moon,
While sea turtles crooned a comical tune.
With flippers and fins, they put on a show,
And the gulls above giggled, "What a circus below!"

The Siren's Silent Call

There once was a siren with quite a strange voice,
Who chirped like a bird, oh what a weird choice!
Her fishy admirers just swam away fast,
Leaving her singing alone, such a blast!

She tried rock and roll, and also some blues,
But all that she got were some seaweed shoes.
With laughter and bubbles, she found her own beat,
In depths where the sea critters danced on their feet.

Nautical Dreams in Silent Waters

In silent waters where dreams come to life,
A shrimp ran for office, much to the wife's strife.
He promised clean currents and seas free of trash,
While jellyfish giggled, "He's gone in a flash!"

The whales enjoyed movies, while squids filmed the show,
With popcorn made of plankton, floating in tow.
As sea cucumbers joined in the play,
The depths burst with laughter, wafting away!

Legends of the Midnight Sea

At midnight hour, the fish conspire,
To play tricks on sailors, which they admire.
Jellyfish glow like disco balls,
While octopuses prank and enjoy their brawls.

A whale dives deep, but forgets his way,
Surfacing to blubber, 'What's today's play?'
Every wave a punchline, every splash a cheer,
Bubbles of laughter echo far and near.

Adventures in the Deep Blue

In the deep blue, a crab found a shoe,
He wore it with style, all mud and goo.
A pufferfish giggled, then swelled up wide,
'This is my look, it's a fashion ride!'

A dolphin zoomed past, whistle in tow,
'Catch me if you can!' he laughed in a row.
But the lazy sea turtle just chuckled back,
'Fast and furious? I could take a snack!'

The Coral Kingdom's Lament

In coral halls where colors abound,
The clownfish joke, with no care profound.
'Why did the sea anemone blush?' they tease,
'It saw the kraken swim by, oh please!'

Yet octopus grumbles, 'I'm tired of this play.
Why can't we have a calm, boring day?'
But the stingrays glide on laughter and light,
Reminding him joy can be found in the night.

Murmurs of the Forgotten Depths

Far in the dark, where the seaweed whispers,
A haggard old anglerfish twirls like a sister.
'Turning every light bulb into a show!'
He grins at the gullible fish below.

Seahorses gossip 'bout bubbles and dreams,
With laughter that dances on soft, velvet streams.
A snapper then quips, 'What's the deal with the gloom?'
'Just add some jokes, and we'll brighten the room!'

Bound by the Depth

A fish in a tux, quite the sight,
Swims a dance in the deep blue night.
With a bow tie of bubbles, he sways,
In the currents, he jigs and he plays.

A crab with a knack for a tune,
Plays the conch, like a jazz buffoon.
Octopus throws a wild, wild bash,
With four arms shaking, making a splash.

The Underwater Library

In the coral shelves, books swim around,
With pages of jelly sticking to the ground.
A whale reads loud from a tale of glee,
While fishes giggle in a seaweed tree.

Librarian squid shushes with flair,
But the clownfish can't stop their silly snare.
Aquatic scholars with sea cucumber snacks,
Plotting to launch the next literary tracks.

Luxuries of the Abyss

Deep in the ocean, where oddities grow,
There's a spa for the fish, with a soft sea flow.
Starfish get massages, and the eel takes a dip,
In a whirlpool of bubbles, they all let it rip.

Seahorses sip on a kelp cocktail,
As jellyfish float in a luminescent veil.
Life in the deep is plush and absurd,
With waves of laughter, you've surely heard.

Tales of Sunken Treasure

A pirate's chest at the bottom lies,
Full of rubber ducks, much to their surprise.
Golden doubloons? Nope, it's just bling,
With pearls that giggle and mermaids that sing.

Diving for hoards, they swim with delight,
Finding odd treasures hidden from sight.
A compass that spins but lacks any clue,
Points towards snacks, a feast in the blue!

Whispers from the Abyss

The fish gossip loud, they can't keep still,
A crab tells a joke that gives them a thrill.
A siren sings off-key, oh what a scene,
Even the seaweed rolls, laughing in green.

With barnacles glued like a stubborn friend,
They tickle the sea turtle—oh, what a trend!
Bubble-blowing clams join the festive parade,
As the octopus juggles, a strange masquerade.

A shipwreck's a party for those who dive deep,
Where mermaids slumber but never do sleep.
A parrotfish cracks jokes with mischief in eyes
While the snail wins the race; oh, what a surprise!

So listen, my friend, to the whispers of blue,
The ocean's a circus, where laughter is true.
Deep down in the chaos, where old meets the new,
Life's one big party, and it's waiting for you!

Secrets of the Sunken World

Down where the shadows play hide and seek,
The turtles read secrets in bubbles unique.
An old ship's captain with a fish for a hat,
Tells tales of lost treasure while tickling a cat.

With starfish in wigs and a dolphin DJ,
They dance to the rhythm of seaweed ballet.
Anemones giggle, they shake and they sway,
And the sea cucumbers just roll with the play.

The treasures are treasures, but none quite compare,
To the laughter and joy in the salty sea air.
Where all that was lost now has found a good home,
And they throw a wild party for all to come roam.

So dive into mischief, let your worries grow small,
In the depths of the ocean, there's laughter for all.
The secrets are silly, delightful, and bright,
In this sunken world, every joke is just right!

Shadows Beneath the Waves

Beneath the waves, where the shadows twist,
A whale tells a story that you can't resist.
A tiny shrimp giggles, it's hard to believe,
It's the funniest fish that you'd ever perceive.

With eels playing tag, and a grouper in glee,
The underwater world's a comical spree.
Octopuses slip on their own tangled arms,
And the playful puffers release their funny charms.

A school of bright fish don't know where to go,
As they try to catch bubbles that float like a show.
The anglerfish winks with a light in its grin,
While jellyfish join in for an elegant spin.

So never forget when you swim in the deep,
The shadows may giggle and secrets they keep.
In the laughter of fish, in their swaying displays.
You'll find joy in the depths, in delightful arrays!

Echoes of the Ocean Floor

On the ocean floor, where the echoes abound,
A clam plays the trumpet, a curious sound.
The sea urchins laugh at the fish with a flair,
As the sea stars roll over, and join in with care.

Coral reefs shimmer, they wink with delight,
As they shower the fish in confetti of light.
The deep sea's a realm where the silly can thrive,
And the kraken's just waving, feeling alive!

With bubbles that pop like balloons on the sea,
Everyone's dancing, so wild and so free.
The whispering waves carry jokes from afar,
As seahorses prance to the tune of a guitar.

So come take a plunge into waters so bright,
Where echoes of laughter fill up every night.
In the depths of the ocean, where chaos is found,
Life's just a party, a joy to surround!

Depths of Enchantment

In the sea where fish wear hats,
Guppies gossip, while octopus chats.
Mermaids juggle shiny shells,
Deep in laughter, the ocean dwells.

A crab with glasses, reading a book,
Claims the tides are a sneaky hook.
He winks and says, 'Take a look here!'
Bubbles float up, tickling our cheer.

The dolphins dance, with springy tails,
While seaweed sings in silly wails.
Even the starfish can't keep still,
They tap their arms with quite the thrill.

So join the party beneath the foam,
In this wet wonderland, we feel at home.
With every giggle, the waves play along,
Life's a splash in this watery throng.

The Song of the Silent Depths

Bubbles pop like tiny balloons,
While seahorses croon silly tunes.
Anemones wave with flappy flair,
Tickling fish with gentle care.

A whale tried to whisper, just for fun,
But sneezed a spray—oh, what a run!
Jellyfish giggle, glowing bright,
They flicker and dive, a whimsical sight.

Octopuses play tag in swirling streams,
Chasing their dreams in wild, wet beams.
They trip on corals, then burst into glee,
Who knew the depths could be so carefree?

With every dive, there's joy to be found,
In the depths where laughter knows no bound.
Bring a friend, let the fun arise,
In this quirky world beneath the skies.

Beneath the Veil of Waves

A fish in pajamas swims with flair,
While shrimps compete for the best hair.
Nemo threw a party, oh what a sight,
Where the seaweed danced through the night.

A clam wearing shoes tried to prance,
But tripped and fell, losing his chance.
The blowfish chuckled, puffed up with pride,
As sea cucumbers joined the ride.

Stars in the ocean, shining with glee,
Whispering secrets, as bright as can be.
A turtle with shades rides waves like a pro,
Saying, 'Life's better when you go with the flow!'

So dive into laughter, let troubles drift,
Down in the depths, there's always a shift.
Join the parade of comedic delight,
Where every splash brings joy to light.

Beneath the Veil of Seafoam

A crab wears a crown, oh what a sight,
Dancing on shells in the pale moonlight.
A fish gives a wink, in a seaweed ball,
While a sneaky eel tries to trip them all.

The clams tell jokes, they chuckle and bide,
A turtle's slow shuffle, no place to hide.
In bubbles they laugh, with glee in their hearts,
As sea cucumbers make silly arts.

An octopus juggles pearls with a flair,
While a clownfish practices his best hair.
Acting like stars in a watery play,
Life's a real giggle beneath the bay.

The waves bring the giggles from deep down below,
Where seahorses prance in a marvelous show.
So dive in the fun, let the bubbles burst,
In the dance of the depths, it's laughter that's cursed.

Constellations of the Sunken Stars

In the brine, we see fish with glasses on,
Reading old maps of what's gone and drawn.
A whale whispers secrets of treasure and fun,
While dolphins laugh gleefully, always on the run.

Starfish debate if they're one or five,
With a wink to the turtle, who seems quite alive.
They sketch in the sand the constellations,
While anemones sway with great celebrations.

A parrotfish sings with a voice like a bell,
As clowns trade impressions that don't go so well.
An old anchor grumbles, stuck under the tide,
But the blarney of seals makes him swell with pride.

With laughter like bubbles all floating around,
The underwater circus spins round and round.
Embrace the whimsy—the watery jest,
In the realm of the depths, find joy and invest!

The Depths' Silent Guardians

The hermit crabs plot with shells for their coats,
Guardians of secrets, they chuckle like goats.
A lionfish pouts, all spines and no charm,
While a school of small minnows weave tales of alarm.

A grouper tells stories of big fishy fears,
While snappers erupt into giggles and cheers.
The rocks hold their breath, as if in a trance,
When a playful anglerfish joins in the dance.

With echoes of laughter that bounce off the reef,
A sea urchin grins, though he's hidden in grief.
Fiddler crabs wave and then wave goodbye,
As the currents of laughter drift swiftly by.

The depths are alive with a vibrant parade,
Where whispers of humor through bubbles cascade.
Let the jests of the sea be your daily delight,
For even the gloom has its pie-in-the-sky light.

Navigating the Dark Waters

In waters so dark, where the lanternfish glow,
A pirate's lost parrot puts on quite a show.
With jokes about krakens, and tales gone astray,
The sea frogs all croak in a ribbity way.

Navigating shadows, with giggles in tow,
A whiting finds seaweed that tickles his toe.
He slips and he slides, it's a slippery plight,
While a wise old turtle rolls eyes in delight.

With sonar as ears, they share clever quips,
While a catfish pursues his fantastical trips.
And treasure maps scribbled with joy and some wine,
Make the dark waters glimmer and shine.

So join in the revels of flotation and fun,
Where laughter is plenty and worries are none.
Through dark and through light, may your journey be bright,
In the depths of the seas where humor takes flight.

Ghostlights at Midnight

Beneath the waves where shadows play,
Ghostlights dance in a merry fray.
They tickle fish with flicks of glee,
Making seaweed giggle, oh so free.

A crab in a top hat takes a bow,
While octopuses sing with a wow!
The bubbles burp with laughter bright,
As the sea creatures party through the night.

Turtles wear glasses, reading the tide,
While sardines swim in synchronized pride.
A whale's joke brings waves of cheer,
Echoing laughter for all to hear.

So if you roam near the ocean's glee,
Watch out for fish with a sense of spree.
In the ghostly glow where secrets unfold,
You'll find the silly stories long told.

Currents of Solitude

In the depths, where silence reigns,
Bubbles giggle, releasing chains.
Lonely seahorses play hide and seek,
In a game that's anything but meek.

A fish with a bowtie spins round and round,
While jellyfish drift with no care found.
Anemones chuckle at the swimming pass,
As the currents tickle, the seaweed laughs.

A deep sea clam tries to tell a joke,
But the shyness makes him choke.
Fish giggle as they swim on by,
In this underwater comedy, oh my!

So if you find yourself feeling blue,
Dive where the currents know what to do.
For beneath the waves, the fun's unbound,
In the solitude of laughter, joy is found.

Forgotten Secrets of the Salty Depths

In the briny deep, where wonders stir,
Secrets of laughter soon concur.
A sunken ship with socks galore,
Makes the fossil fish laugh and adore.

Mermaids gossip with crabs in tow,
About the treasure they once did know.
They drink from pearls, a bubbly brew,
And share old tales that feel brand new.

A treasure chest filled with socks and hats,
Looks quite lovely to plump little spats.
The sea cucumbers nod with delight,
While barnacles tap dance through the night.

So dive on down if you seek some fun,
In the salty depths, the laughter's begun.
Forgotten secrets float without strife,
In the ocean's embrace, discover new life.

The Path of the Drowned Sailor

Once there was a sailor, bold and keen,
Who wore bright stripes and a laugh so clean.
He slipped on a fish, went for a dive,
Now he strolls where jellyfish thrive.

He tells the clams of his daring fate,
As they giggle and spread tales that wait.
With gullible gulls following close behind,
They search for his heart, so heartily kind.

The starfish chuckle, "Where's your crew?"
The sailor waves, "They're lost in the blue!"
A sea turtle smirks, "Let's make it a race,"
As the laughter floats through this watery place.

So if you wander the pathways deep,
Remember the sailor who took a leap.
In the depths where the funny stories flow,
You'll find his spirit, just let it show.

Echoes in the Dark Waters

Fish in tuxedos swim with glee,
Nibbling snacks from the sea!
Crabs throw a dance party at night,
Bubbles burst in sheer delight.

Octopus plays the dizzy drums,
While clam shells nod to the tunes!
With every wave, a joke is told,
The ocean sparkles, bright and bold.

Eels in bow ties twist and twirl,
Sardines whirl around in a swirl!
Lobsters laugh, 'Oh let's not drown!'
Tickling the seaweed, they clown around.

When dawn breaks, the humor fades,
Fish wear shades in sunlit glades!
But night will come, fun will revive,
In dark waters, they all jive!

Shadows Beneath the Waves

A jellyfish with a lightbulb hat,
Floats around, 'Aren't I sleek and fat?'
Seahorses giggle in tiny packs,
While anchor fish plot to sneak some snacks.

Starfish claim they're having a spa,
While barnacles sing, 'Oh, ta-da!'
Clownfish juggle coral with flair,
As squids scribble doodles in the air.

Whale sounds echo like a tune,
'Are we dining? What's for noon?'
With blubbers loud and tails that flap,
They dive for burgers, a tasty slap!

As shadows dance in the blue expanse,
Creatures form a merry prance.
Each ripple hides laughter, it's true,
In depths so deep, it's a laugh or two!

The Siren's Call

A siren sings with a voice so sweet,
Fish drop their tools and tap their feet.
Her hair's a mess, with shells galore,
They giggle, 'What's she singing for?'

With scales that shimmer, a sight so bright,
She croons about an ocean kite!
"Who needs a prince?" she quips in jest,
"Let's have a fish feast, it's the best!"

Cranky crabs refuse to join,
'We're busy here—this shell's a coin!'
But laughing gulls swoop down to play,
Siren's charm wins them all, hooray!

Each note she sings causes a splash,
As fish dive deep in a colorful dash.
Under the waves, a party unfolds,
Where strumming tunes break ocean molds!

Chronicles of the Ocean Floor

Beneath the waves, where laughter sneaks,
Anemones whisper their funny peaks.
With wiggly worms telling tall tales,
And grumpy fish with cloudy gales.

Coral castles with moat-like rings,
Flounders play chess with odd-fish kings.
A crab narrates tales of lost socks,
While clams are busy making blocks!

Zany dolphins dart to and fro,
They join in on the underwater show!
With flips and tricks, they steal the scene,
As kelp waves dance, all lush and green.

At the close of day, the tales unwind,
Each creature chuckles, no worries in mind.
For in these depths, the fun won't miss,
In ocean chronicles, laughter's bliss!

Nightfall in the Deep

When darkness falls, fish start to dance,
They wear tiny hats, and prance in a trance.
Crabs join the party, snapping their claws,
As jellyfish giggle, defying all laws.

An octopus juggles with some shiny shells,
While sea turtles whisper, sharing their spells.
The starfish are clapping, their arms on the floor,
As seahorses twirl in a waltz to the shore.

A deep-sea clownfish tells a joke or two,
The anglerfish laughs, but it's hard to see who!
With bubbles of laughter, the gang can't stop,
In the night-time abyss, they dance till they plop.

As dawn breaks, the fun must come to an end,
With sleepy goodnights, like a foam-covered friend.
So when night returns, don't forget the parade,
Beneath waves, the laughter in darkness is made.

The Enchanted Seaweed Grove

In seaweed forests with tendrils so bright,
Fish play hide-and-seek, it's a marvelous sight.
A sea cucumber, shy, hides under a leaf,
While seahorses plot a clumsy mischief.

A crab conducts music with sticks on a rock,
Pufferfish puff up—what a pop-culture shock!
The octopus paints pictures in colors so wild,
Of mermaids and pirates, oh, nature's own child!

The seaweed sways as the laughter ignites,
A narwhal arrives, causing frightful delights.
He tells tall tales of things deep and round,
While the giggles of fish echo all around.

As twilight descends, they'll all wave goodbye,
In the enchanted grove where wonders can lie.
With silly shenanigans, they're a merry crew,
Beneath swaying seaweed, they bid a fond adieu.

Beneath the Moonlit Waves

Under the moon, where the fishes all glow,
A dolphin does tricks, putting on quite a show.
The clams start to sing, with shells as their mic,
While shrimp spin around, just like on a bike.

Anemones sway, swishing soft in the tide,
As a goofball sea turtle, with friends, takes a ride.
The sounds of the sea form a musical blend,
As the fish in the moonlight create a new trend.

A far-off conch shell cackles, "Look at that!"
A starfish strikes poses, and much to our chat—
It floats like a diva, all arms in the air,
While the sea cucumbers gasp, but really don't care!

When morning light breaks, they'll sleep off the fun,
Exhausted from giggles, all huddled in one.
So when night rolls back and the moon starts to beam,
Know the sea's full of laughter, it's all a big dream!

Forgotten Coral Gardens

In forgotten gardens beneath vibrant skies,
Anemones tickle, while clownfish all pries.
The coral is giggling, a sight to behold,
As the guppies recount all their treasures of gold.

A group of small minnows is playing charades,
While a grumpy old snail only sits in the shades.
The sea urchins chuckle, in spiky delight,
"It's a fancy parade, well, that's quite the sight!"

A lobster with antics, showing off his new shoes,
Clumsy but happy, he's got nothing to lose.
Amidst all the silliness, a mermaid appears,
With a belly full of laughter, she dances, it cheers!

As twilight descends, the gardens will sigh,
With whispers of joy as the sea creatures fly.
In forgotten coral, where laughter won't cease,
The magic of humor brings cycles of peace.

The Lure of Hidden Currents

Beneath the waves so sly and smart,
They play at games, a watery art.
Fish in top hats, a ball they throw,
With jellyfish waltzing to and fro.

Crabs don their coats, the oysters cheer,
A seaweed band plays tunes we hear.
Bubble-blowing sea turtles grin,
While seahorses tango, let's begin!

But watch out for sharks with a penchant for pranks,
They'll tickle your fins and steal all your flanks.
Just when you think you've found your groove,
They're off with your snack, making you move!

So come take a dive into waters broad,
Where laughter in currents makes all feel awed.
With every splash, a giddy affair,
Waves of joy ripple through salty air.

Depth Charge of Past Lives

In olden days, I was a whale,
Eating krill like a grand-scale tale.
Now I'm a clownfish, all dressed up,
Telling sea stories in a kiddie cup.

I once ruled the depths, a fearsome shark,
City lights sparkled like a lark.
Now I'm stuck in coral, quite the plight,
Pretending to be a rock each night!

Octopus teacher with ink for the brain,
Reciting my life like a scholarly train.
But my students just giggle, swim away fast,
Sneaky little squids, they have a blast!

At the end of the day, I'll take my rest,
Dreaming of waves once fiercely blessed.
Oh, past lives dance like bubbles so bright,
In the ocean of laughter, deep with delight.

Shipwrecked Echoes

A ship once sailed with dreams so grand,
Now on the seabed, it's just a band.
With echoes of sailors singing loud,
Mermaids are found in a playful crowd.

"Hey there, matey, where's your gold?"
Sardines giggle as stories unfold.
"Sunken treasures are just old hats,
With rafts of jelly and singing brats!"

Duck and dive with barnacle pals,
Playing tag with puzzled squalls.
But watch for the kraken, near the wreck,
He's just a softy, a gentle speck!

So gather 'round for a laugh or two,
The ocean's whispers bring stories anew.
Each floundering fish has a tale to tell,
In shipwrecked echoes, we all swell!

Undercurrents of Memory

Bubbles pop like jokes from the past,
In currents of time, good memories blast.
Seaweed sweeps with whispers of glee,
Of clams that do cartwheels and dance with the sea.

Anemones jig with a flick and a spin,
While dolphins debate who will win.
"Remember the time we flipped in the air?"
"Or was it your tail that gave a scare?"

Echoes of laughter, a splash in the dark,
Crooning and cooing, sequential spark.
Fishy friends gather, the tide brings us near,
Sharing secrets that only we hear.

In the swirl of the deep, joy freely flows,
Smiles like bubbles in water that glows.
For in this vast ocean, we find our way,
With undercurrents where memories play.

Legends Adrift

In waters wide, a fish did boast,
He claimed he swam from coast to coast.
But when asked how, he spun a tale,
'It's all in the flip of my finned tail!'

The octopus heard, with a wink of an eye,
'You couldn't swim, not even to die!'
With eight arms crossed, he laughed so loud,
At the fishy claims of being so proud.

A crab scuttled by, with pinchers held high,
'I've seen you splash; now tell me, why lie?'
The fish just shrugged, 'It's fun to pretend,
In this great ocean, where tales never end.'

So, the legends grew, like bubbles a-float,
Wild stories of fish in a miniature boat.
Each creature in blue, with a giggle would share,
About the grand fish who darted through air!

The Forgotten Reef

Deep down where the turtles wear crowns,
Lived a sea sponge who made silly frowns.
He'd dance every night under glowing moons,
With a jellyfish band playing goofy tunes.

A clam yelled out, 'You look quite absurd!'
Yet the sponge just swayed, undeterred.
'Are you not jealous of my splendid moves?
I bring the party, which everyone grooves!'

The parrotfish chuckled, with colors so bright,
'Your wiggle's unique, like a fish in a fright!'
But the sponge just twirled, in an oceanic glee,
'This reef is my stage; come dance with me!'

And so every night, in that vibrant domain,
Creatures would gather, forgetting their pain.
For laughter resounded, in bubbles and cheer,
At the wild underwater fun of the year!

Echoes of the Old Shipwright

In the harbor's mist, an old boat creaked,
Its captain was grumpy and far from chic.
He talked to the gulls, saying 'Listen up,
My ship's not a bathtub, it's seaworthy sup!'

But the seagulls cawed, with a swoop so sly,
'You call it a vessel? Oh me, oh my!'
Every wave that rocked, they made fun of his brag,
While he patched up the hull, with an old rag tag.

Then one day a storm rolled in with a roar,
The captain stood firm, a legend of yore.
But when lightning struck, and the waves got bold,
The ship flew apart — oh, say what a sight!

He swam to the shore, and shook off the spray,
'Next time I'll make sure to just stay away!'
Now the whispers were hushed, 'What a sailor so grand,
Who talks to the gulls, but can't take a stand!'

Riddles of the Deep Sea

A wise old squid sat snug on a rock,
Spinning riddles that tickled the clock.
'What swims in pairs, yet cannot be caught?
I'll tell you a secret; oh, it's more than a thought!

A clownfish grinned, fiddling with hue,
'Is it two-headed eels? Or just me and my crew?'
'Finding the answer is half of the fun,'
The squid laughed aloud, 'Now come, everyone!'

A grouper chimed in, with a wiggle and sway,
'Is it something from only the dark underwater bay?'
'You're getting closer, but think a bit wide,'
The squid twisted ink, as the fish swam inside.

Finally, a shrimp, with a pinch of delight,
Said softly, 'It's friendship — our bond tight as night!'
'Well done!' cried the squid, ink spraying with glee
'In this ocean of riddles, we are truly free!'

Shadows Play in the Reef

In the reef where shadows dance,
Fish wear hats and take their chance.
Starfish play cards on the seabed,
While octopuses share tales they've read.

A clownfish juggles bubbles bright,
Sardines spin in a silly flight.
The seaweed sways to music strange,
As giggles boom through paths of change.

Crabs in suits strut with some sass,
Puffers puff and watch the grass.
Turtles cheer, 'You've got this, mate!'
It's a party at marine fate!

So when you dive, don't be misled,
Join the fun where laughter's spread.
For in the depths, humor's alive,
Underwater, they thrive and jive.

Beneath the Surface: A Nautical Odyssey

Beneath the waves, there's quite a show,
Mermaids sipping on pearly flow.
Seahorses race with a costume flair,
While dolphins dance without a care.

A whale blows bubbles in a tune,
Fish form a line, they want to croon.
The jellyfish boast their glowing lights,
They twist and twirl on watery nights.

Anchors are tossed like frisbees, sure,
While barnacles play bingo for more!
A message in a bottle, what will it tell?
Just a fish seeking out his shell!

Mysteries abound in this wet domain,
Where everything floats, nothing's plain.
So enjoy the depths, let laughter flow,
In this aquatic circus, all steal the show!

Whispers from the Abyss

Down in the deep where whispers call,
Ghostly fish play peekaboo with all.
A turtle tells jokes, slow and sly,
While grouper chuckles, oh me, oh my!

With gurgles and gaggles, bubbles bound,
Even the rocks are laughing around.
A crab comes out wearing shades of blue,
Says, 'Can you believe the view?'

Anglerfish flaunt their glow-in-the-dark,
In shadows hide, they trick and spark.
Every echo brings a chuckle or two,
In the abyss, the fun's never through!

So dive right in, embrace the fray,
In these depths, hilarity's on display.
With each submerged grin, let worries cease,
The abyss is alive, dancing with peace!

Secrets of the Sunken Realm

In the wrecks where treasures rest,
Fish play hide and seek, no jest.
Old anchors wink from muddy beds,
While sea cucumbers talk with heads.

A pirate parrot tells tall tales,
Of lost gold and giant snails.
The octopus stirs a pot of stew,
While clams prepare a dance or two.

"Look!" says the eel, "I've got moves!"
Grinning sharks show off their grooves.
It's a shindig beneath the waves,
Where laughter reigns and humor saves.

Secrets swirl in the salty air,
With fishy giggles everywhere.
In the sunken realm, let joy prevail,
For in the depths, we tell the tale!

Castaways and Echoes

A sailor lost in a sea of glee,
Found a fish that spoke to him free.
"I've got your shoes, they fit me right!"
He chuckled hard, what a silly sight!

A crab joined in with a clam-chop clap,
"Hey buddy, don't fall into a nap!"
They danced on waves, quite the odd crew,
Under the sun, with horizons so blue.

A mermaid giggled, splashed her tail,
"You missed my show, you must set sail!"
"Apologies, dear, I just lost my hat,"
The sailor replied, in this joyful spat!

Together they laughed, in ocean's spree,
Castaways singing, wild and free!
With seaweed crowns and pretzel charms,
They made merry, with no alarms!

The Forbidden Trench

Deep down below, where no fish tread,
Lurks a funny beast with a bright red head.
"Do not come here!" the sign did say,
But who could resist such a curious play?

A turtle strolled in, wearing a bow,
"This trench is a blast, give it a go!"
With jellyfish glow, they lit up the night,
A party erupted, what a crazy sight!

They sang with bubbles, the murky breeze,
A dance-off began, with wobbly knees.
The beast just smiled, with a wink and a cheer,
"Join the fun, friends, let's drink some sea beer!"

So laughter bubbled in the watery lair,
In the forbidden trench, joys danced in the air.
No rules to follow, just friends everywhere,
A splash of humor, dread turned to flair!

Serenity Below

Where silence reigns and bubbles burst,
A whale told jokes, it was quite a first!
"Why don't fish play cards, you see?"
"They're afraid of the deck, it's too fishy!"

The octopus groaned, then he cracked a grin,
"Let's make this deep dive an epic win!"
They played underwater charades all day,
With everyone laughing, what a grand play!

A seahorse galloped, all dressed in gold,
"I'm the king of the depths, or so I'm told!"
They cheered him on, it was all in good fun,
A kingdom of laughter, where all could run!

As sunbeams tickled the ocean floor,
Serenity bloomed, what a splendid roar!
With humor and joy, they danced with delight,
In the depths of the sea, oh what a sight!

Drowned Musings

In the sea of dreams where bubbles float,
A fish scribbles notes in a tiny boat.
"Today I had a grand old chat,
With a dolphin who swears he's part acrobat!"

Each stroke of his fin was a laugh on the page,
"The squid in the corner is stuck in a rage!"
He doodled a scene of mermaid ballet,
While trying to dodge a splashy, blue ray!

A crab strutted by with a top hat on,
"I'm here to perform, the show must go on!"
They cheered as he waved, a comedic delight,
In the midst of the depths, on that whimsical night!

From coral reefs, came a raucous cheer,
"More jokes, more dance, bring them all near!"
In drowned musings, the sea found its beat,
In the laughter below, joy was complete!

The Forgotten Ones

In the depths, where shadows play,
Forgotten souls dance night and day.
With silly hats and shoes askew,
They juggle fish and sing a tune.

Their laughter echoes, a bubbly sound,
As they tumble and trip on the ocean ground.
One breaks a shell, a comical crash,
While seahorses cheer and make a splash!

The seaweed sways with a giggly sway,
Whispering secrets of their silly play.
An octopus joins, with a wink so sly,
Inking the mischief as time slips by.

Amidst the sea, in this joyous place,
The forgotten ones find their happy space.
With jokes and pranks, they rule the tide,
In their world of whimsy, they take great pride.

The Unseen Depth

Beneath the waves, a secret lair,
Where creatures giggle without a care.
Invisible antics, a playful spree,
Adventures await, come dance with me!

A crab with glasses reads a fishy book,
While a slippery eel plays hide and hook.
Is that a mermaid with a bubble wand?
Or a dolphin doing the conga—how fond!

The narwhals giggle, their tusks all aglow,
In this realm where the jesters all flow.
Hiding from sailors, a playful game,
The unseen depth, never quite the same.

A treasure chest bursts with laughter and cheer,
Filled with odd socks and an old rubber spear.
In this world, where jesters reside,
Every ripple brings joy, like a fun-filled ride.

Creatures of the Abyss

In the dark, where the sea life thrives,
Creatures with humor lead double lives.
A grouchy fish with a bubble beard,
Throws parties every night—he's never feared!

A starfish juggles pearls and shells,
While a jellyfish rings its squishy bells.
Whales crack jokes in the muddy blue,
Their laughter echoes, as if they knew.

An angler fish with a wacky grin,
Shows off his light like it's a sin.
The squid joins in, with a dance so slick,
They twirl together, a humorous trick!

In this abyss, where fun is the key,
Creatures unite in jubilee.
With gags and pranks, they shine like gold,
In the depths of laughter, their joy unfolds.

Relics of the Depth

Forgotten relics on the ocean floor,
Tell tales of laughter, parties, and more.
A rusty anchor with a mustache bold,
Confides in the shells of the stories told.

Bottles bobbing; treasure or trash?
Inside are messages, funny and brash.
One bottle says, 'Don't eat the nightshades!'
While another warns of overly sly mermaids!

A sunken ship that's now a fun park,
With a slide made from wood, quite the spark.
The fish are swinging, high on a line,
While crabs play tag, feeling mighty fine.

Relics of laughter, in watery dreams,
With whispers of fun and sea creature schemes.
In the depths they hide, with joy in their hearts,
Crafting a world where humor imparts.

Chasing the Kraken's Shadow

In murky waters, tentacles swirl,
With a splash and a giggle, I give it a whirl.
"Catch me, you beast, if you dare to run,"
But the kraken just laughs, having too much fun.

I chased it through shipwrecks, old and decayed,
Past pirate bones, where sea cucumbers played.
It turned every corner with style and flair,
While I tripped on a fish and got splashed everywhere.

We danced 'neath the waves, in a water ballet,
I twirled like a dolphin, the kraken would sway.
With a wink and a nod, it dove down below,
Leaving me giggling, with nowhere to go.

So next time you see a shadow in the blue,
Remember the kraken's a jokester too.
In the depths of the sea, where few dare to tread,
There's laughter and mischief 'mongst creatures well-fed.

Melodies of the Mariana Trench

In the depths of the trench, fish sing a tune,
With bubbles and bubbles, they dance to the moon.
A crab plays the drums on a shipwreck's plight,
While the mantle rocks gently, a whimsical sight.

A squid plays the flute, with a curious flair,
While seahorses prance without a single care.
They harmonize bubbles that rise to the waves,
In the oceanic concert, sea life misbehaves.

"Watch out for the shark!" a goblin fish croaks,
But laughter erupts, as they share all their jokes.
With seaweed as microphones, they belt out with glee,
No grandeur or grandeur, just pure jubilee.

So if you should dive to the ocean's deep core,
Keep your ears open wide for the underwater score.
For the melodies flow through the currents, you see,
A funny aquatic symphony, wild and free.

Secrets of the Starry Thalassia

In Thalassia's glow, a glowworm will jest,
"Want to see secrets? Come join the quest!"
With shimmering lights, it wiggles and waves,
While fish trade tall tales of old sunken graves.

A starfish named Stan shared gossip so sly,
"How many legs does a lobster supply?"
With laughter erupting from an eel's quick strike,
They join in the fun, as they tease and they pipe.

With jellyfish chuckles that swirl through the night,
They float in the currents, a colorful sight.
"Did you hear about Barry, the crab with three claws?
He dances like lightning and claps with applause!"

In the currents of Thalassia, laughter will rise,
A circus beneath, filled with playful surprise.
So swim down below, where friendships are deep,
For secrets and giggles are treasures to keep.

Oceanic Lore

The tales of the deep are often a riot,
With bumps and with splashes—a slippery diet.
There's a fish with a hat and a crab in a tie,
Who claim they could outswim the fastest smart fly.

The dolphin jokes loudly, "Who needs a ship?"
As it spins through the waves with a flip and a sip.
A turtle swims slowly, in no kind of rush,
While a sea snail's offering delicious sea mush.

The secrets they share, while the currents do flow,
Of octopi playing cards, hidden below.
With winks and with nudges, they chuckle away,
For in the ocean's lore, it's a comical play.

So dive with a grin, and don't take it serious,
The funny fish stories will leave you delirious.
With each splash and each giggle, there's so much to explore,
In the depths of the ocean, there's always much more.

Songs from the Bottomless Chasm

In the chasm where echoes dance,
Fish wear hats, and eels prance.
Octopus chefs whip up delights,
Jellyfish throwing glittery fights.

A whale with jokes, a comic star,
His punchlines travel near and far.
Sea turtles giggle, rolling on the sea,
While crabs snap claws, 'Come laugh with me!'

Starfish in pajamas, they tease and play,
Sardines swirl in a disco ballet.
Coral reefs chime in a cheerful tune,
As bubbles rise up, a bubbly cartoon.

Down in the depths, where the sun's quite shy,
Sea cucumbers share a pie in the sky.
With every splash and giggle, we see,
The ocean's just one big comedy spree.

Chronicles of the Deep Currents

Currents swirl with quirky tales,
Where fish ride waves in tiny sails.
Clownfish jesters in the coral court,
Make laughter echo, oh what sport!

A dolphin whispers, 'What's the news?'
A sea horse says, 'I lost my shoes!'
The seaweed sways with glee and grace,
As waves tickle the fish's face.

In undercurrents, secrets slosh,
Where turtles breakdance and do the wash.
Sharks throw parties, all fun and cheer,
Inviting everyone from far and near.

Anemones wear their best bow ties,
While stingrays glide with silly sighs.
In deep blue waters, bright and bold,
The currents weave a yarn of gold.

Voices of the Ocean's Heart

Under the waves, the sea does sing,
With crabs and clams embracing spring.
Oysters gossip, in shells they confide,
While fish trade tales of their wild ride.

A mermaid strums on a coral harp,
As dolphins tease with their nimble dart.
Each splash and flip, a giggle in the night,
As sea stars twinkle, shining bright.

Tidal waves tap dance, a foam-top show,
While sea cucumbers steal the flow.
A sand dollar sings, 'Life's a blast!'
With every ripple, memories cast.

Crab come dressed in a polka-dot bow,
"Who's the silliest creature? Come on, let's go!"
The ocean's murmurs fill the room,
With laughter echoing, dispelling gloom.

Mysteries in the Abyssal Realm

In the deep where shadows play,
Creatures giggle in a wobbly way.
Anglerfish sparkle with lights aglow,
Singing songs of the hidden flow.

Squids with secrets, they plot and scheme,
As they swirl around in a colorful dream.
Cuttlefish chuckle, showing their hues,
As they change colors and share the news.

In the abyss where the laughter roams,
Ghostly fish build whimsical homes.
Their laughter bubbles, echoing clear,
In a world that thrives on joy and cheer.

Giant squids do the limbo low,
While fish make waves in a fluid show.
The darkness shines with humor bright,
In this watery land of pure delight.

Journey Through the Blue Abyss

In the depths, a fish wore a tie,
But forgot how to swim, oh my!
Dancing with eels in a swirl,
While jellyfish giggled and twirled.

A crab flipped burgers with flair,
Selling sandwiches to a whale, beware!
Octopus chefs in the galley churn,
Making gourmet meals with a twist and aurn.

A clam told jokes about pearls,
While sea turtles flipped in whirls.
With laughter echoing so bold,
Even the sea cucumbers rolled.

So join the parties under the waves,
Where laughter is what the ocean craves.
In the blue abyss, fun's the decree,
A splashy spectacle, wild and free!

The Ocean's Hidden Treasury

Beneath the waves, there's treasure unkept,
A sock from Neptune, where it leapt!
Goldfish wearing crowns of old,
Swapping their stories and tales of gold.

A pirate parrot on a diet cake,
Danced with crabs till the dawn's wake.
Turtles held cards in a game of chance,
While starfish cheered them on, what a dance!

Mermaids giggled at fishy pajamas,
Kissing on fins, oh what a drama!
The sunken chests were filled with glee,
As treasures sparkled so lavishly.

So dive right in, join the spree,
In the ocean's hoard, there's mirth for thee!
With goodies and laughter in the sea's glow,
Unlikely friendships steal the show!

Silence Amidst the Waves

In the quiet, a sea anemone snores,
While wise old turtles share ancient lore.
A clam with a book tried to read:
"Shhh! Don't disturb me—I'm in the lead!"

A muffled laugh through bubbles broke free,
As fish tickled each other, oh what a spree!
The jellyfish juggled with glee,
In silence, they giggled beneath the sea.

Catch the humor in fishy whispers,
A conch shell choir with save-the-dippers!
They all fall silent—who made that noise?
Just the sea otters flaunting their toys!

So let's embrace the silence profound,
Where laughter hides and fun is found.
In the depths where whispers swirl and play,
Join the jesters in their silent ballet!

Uncharted Waters of Wonder

In waters unknown, a whale took a dive,
Hoping to spy on a fish that can jive.
With dolphins in tow, they danced with delight,
Creating new waves under the moonlight.

A sea urchin donned a head to a hat,
Proclaiming itself as 'the ruler of that.'
Starfish were voting on dancing the conga,
While pouty puffer-fish puffed like a mongo.

Amidst coral reefs that shimmer and blink,
A moody old grouper began to think.
What if he painted with colors so bright?
Would he get invited to the next big night?

So chart your course where laughter's the key,
In these uncharted waters full of glee.
For wonders await where the silliness flows,
In the depths of the ocean where laughter grows!

Dreams Drowned in Tides

A fish wore a hat, quite bizarre,
He danced on the waves, like a star.
The crab called him silly, with a scoff,
But the fish just danced, and did not take off.

The octopus laughed, with eight arms in glee,
Said, "Join the sea party! Come, dance with me!"
They twirled in the foam, without a care,
Till a whale gave a splash, they forgot the air.

A jellyfish grooved, glowin' in style,
The anchors were groaning, "Just stay for a while!"
But the waves were so strong, they just couldn't land,
And the fish and the crab joined the ocean band.

So fins flipped in humor, the bubbles flew high,
As laughter echoed under the sky.
In a world full of quirks, beneath the blue,
The dreams drifted by, with each splash anew.

The Guardian of the Abyss

Deep in the ocean, lives a strange guy,
With a mustache that tickles, oh my, oh my!
He guards all the treasures, the pearls, the gold,
Yet prefers telling jokes to the stories of old.

A sea turtle approached, quite wise and slow,
Asked, "Why so funny? What's the show?"
The guardian chuckled, "Why, life is a play!
I'd rather crack jokes than let worries sway!"

A pufferfish puffed, all prickly and bold,
Joined in the laughter, the stories retold.
"Why did the clam not share her pearl?"
"Because she was shy, and it just made her swirl!"

With bubbles of giggles, they roamed through the blue,
Zany creatures beneath, oh, what a view!
In the depths where they dwell, amidst laughs galore,
The guardian guards both the treasures and more.

The Heart of the Ocean's Silence

In the heart of the sea, where it's quiet and deep,
Lived a snail with a shell, who could never sleep.
He dreamed of a chorus, so grand and so bright,
But the only sound heard was a fish with a bite.

A seahorse swayed by, sporting starry shades,
Said, "Why not create your own serenade?"
The snail gave a grin, with a wink and a sigh,
"I'll gather the critters, and we'll amplify!"

So they called every fish, from the big to the small,
To sing in the night, oh, they'd have a ball!
But one fish forgot, and kept swimming away,
So they just used a clam as a makeshift DJ.

Bass from the clams, and the seaweed swayed,
With laughter and fun, their worries delayed.
The silence was shattered, joy echoed so clear,
In the depths of the ocean, the heart brought them cheer.

Mysteries Beneath the Surface

What's that beneath waves, with a glimmer so bright?
Is it treasure or trouble, that swims out of sight?
A shrimp said, "It's secrets, from ancient days past!"
While a dolphin just laughed, saying, "Let's hope it lasts!"

The tangles of seaweed became tales of lore,
Each twist held a joke, that was hard to ignore.
The anglerfish grinned, with a light in his smile,
"Who knew depths could giggle? Just wait a short while!"

A pod of whales joined, with voices so grand,
Telling tall tales of the sea's shifting sand.
But one fish piped up, with a cheeky retort,
"Are these just grand fables or fishy support?"

So down in the deep, where the silliness swirls,
They spun out their stories, as laughter unfurls.
Mysteries linger, but one thing is clear,
In the depths they found humor, and that brought them cheer.

Fragments of Fluid Dreams

Amidst the bubbles, fish do dance,
A giggling octopus in a trance.
With every splash, a joke unfolds,
The tales of brine and seaweed molds.

A clam confides, "I'm quite the chef,
I bake in shells, hope for a clef!"
The sea snails race, but they're too slow,
In ocean currents, they steal the show.

A jellyfish jests, 'I float and glide,
You humans wish you were this wide!'
With laughter trapped in a bubble's thread,
The depths of humor swirl instead.

So if you dive to watery lands,
Watch for the critters with funny plans.
For in the depths, where dreams unfold,
The frolics of the sea, pure gold.

Currents of Old Lore

The crab once claimed he's king of the bay,
But a wise old fish said, 'Not today!'
They whisper secrets in gurgling delight,
Of underwater creatures in jest every night.

A sea turtle took a selfie too bold,
'Just look at the pose, I'm a sight to behold!'
With a wink and a smile, the dolphins all cheer
As sardines giggle, 'We're still in the clear!'

The rays sing songs that make bubbles pop,
With tunes so fine, you'll never want to stop.
While sea cucumbers roll with the tide,
Sharing their jokes with cozy pride.

So drift on the waves, let laughter descend,
In currents of humor, the fun never ends.
From coral to kelp, let good vibes explore,
In these liquid realms, there's always more.

The Mystic Waters

In waters deep, the dolphins play,
With flips and dives, they steal the day.
The seaweed sways in a goofy way,
Tickling the crabs as they shout, 'Hooray!'

An anglerfish with a glowing grin,
Calls out, "Come over, let's spin, spin, spin!'
The squid performs its inky art,
Turning the ocean into a heart.

A hermit crab sports shells of bright hues,
While blushing, admits, 'I've got the blues!'
The conch shell laughs, 'You're quite the ace,
Come join my conga, let's own this place!'

So plunge into depths where humor abounds,
In the mystic waters, joy's the sound.
With each splash, a giggle will bloom,
In the ocean's embrace, there's always room.

The Oath of the Ocean's Depths

A seal's on a mission, says it's a race,
Against the tide, it's quite the chase.
With sea urchins cheering, 'You've got the flair!'
They flip upside down without a care.

The clownfish chuckles from the reef's bright face,
'Laugh now, swim later, that's the pace!'
With bubbles of joy, the waters burst wide,
While starfish sidestep, full of pride.

A fishy affair, the crabs breakdance,
With shells that rattle, they take a stance.
The ocean sways to this rhythmic beat,
As laughter echoes all round the fleet.

Take the pledge to share a grin,
In the deep blue where laughter begins.
For every wave holds a promise of cheer,
An oath of silly, from far and near.

www.ingramcontent.com/pod-product-compliance
Lightning Source LLC
Chambersburg PA
CBHW060144230426
43661CB00003B/565